CONTENTS

Acknowledgements

The author and publishers wish to acknowledge the following photograph sources:

BBC Hulton Picture Library pp 6 left, 12, 13 left, 16, 27, 30, 39, 40, 43; British Museum p 11 bottom; Manchester Public Libraries p 13 right; Mansell Collection pp 11 top, 19; Newcastle-upon-Tyne City Libraries pp 6 right, 6/7, 32; *Punch* pp 18, 45; Tyne and Wear County Council (Sunderland Museum) pp 22, 23, 23, 31; Wellcome Institute Library, London p 47.

PREFACE

The study of history is exciting, whether in a good story well told, a mystery solved by the judicious unravelling of clues, or a study of the men, women and children whose fears and ambitions, successes and tragedies make up the collective memory of mankind.

This series aims to reveal this excitement to pupils through a set of topic books on important historical subjects from the Middle Ages to the present day. Each book contains four main elements: a narrative and descriptive text, lively and relevant illustrations, extracts of contemporary evidence, and questions for further thought and work. Involvement in these elements should provide an adventure which will bring the past to life in the imagination of the pupil.

Each book is also designed to develop the knowledge, skills and concepts so essential to a pupil's growth. It provides a wide, varying introduction to the evidence available on each topic. In handling this evidence, pupils will increase their understanding of basic historical concepts such as causation and change, as well as of more advanced ideas such as revolution and democracy. In addition, their use of basic study skills will be complemented by more sophisticated historical skills such as the detection of bias and the formulation of opinion.

The intended audience for the series is pupils of eleven to sixteen years: it is expected that the earlier topics will be introduced in the first three years of secondary school, while the nineteenth and twentieth century topics are directed towards first examinations.

the **information** store
01603 773114
email: tis@ccn.ac.uk

21 DAY LOAN ITEM

Please return <u>on or before</u> the last date stamped above

A fine will be charged for overdue items

CITY COLLEGE NORWICH

PU████H

H█

Sixth Fo█

M
Macmillan Education

First published 1985
Reprinted 1986, 1987 (twice)

Published by
MACMILLAN EDUCATION LTD
Houndmills, Basingstoke, Hampshire RG21 2XS
and London
Companies and representatives
throughout the world

Printed in Hong Kong

British Library Cataloguing in Publication Data
Tonge, Neil
Cholera and public health.—(History in depth)
1. Cholera, Asiatic—Great Britain—
History—19th century 2. Epidemics—
Great Britain—History—19th century
3. Cholera, Asiatic—Social aspects—
Great Britain
I. Title II. Quincey, Michael III. Series
303.4′85   RA644.C3
ISBN 0-333-35080-4

A PLACE OF DESPAIR

Suppose you board a train and find yourself in a Victorian city as it was in the 1830s. What would it be like?

Many fine shops and offices had been built in city centres. There were covered markets bustling with traders and customers, busy exchanges full of frock-coated businessmen, imposing town halls and clusters of banks. Fine theatres with elegant columns, and new public houses gleaming with polished mahogany and brass were places to attract the rich and prosperous.

But suppose you leave the fashionable city centre and walk down one of the dark alleyways towards the poorer part of the city. You have to pick your way carefully through the piled-up filth and excrement, both human and animal, that litters the narrow streets. Suddenly the silent blackness is broken by a drunken scream and the whimpering of a child lying half-naked under a broken door.

In this part of the city, life is a desperate struggle; a place of despair if you are poor, a place to be avoided if you are prosperous. Of the upper classes, only those with a strong stomach and social conscience explored this unknown territory.

In the city of Newcastle upon Tyne, Dr D.B. Reid submitted a report describing such horrors to the Newcastle Corporation:

necessaries: public toilets

The streets most densely populated by the humbler classes are a mass of filth where the direct rays of the sun never reach. In some of the courts I have noticed heaps of filth, amounting to 20 or 50 tons, which, when it rains penetrate into some of the cellar dwellings. A few public necessaries have been built, but too few to serve the population. To take a single example of one of the more extreme cases shown to me when visiting them during the day, a room was noticed with scarcely any furniture and in which there were two children of two and three years of age absolutely naked, except for a little straw to protect them from the cold, and in which they could not have been discovered in the darkness if they had not been heard to cry.

Piggeries were also pointed out to me which added their offence to the causes already mentioned.

privies: toilets

The absence of dustbins was everywhere a cause of great annoyance, and no such activity horrified me more than the attempt to keep the refuse of privies for the purpose of selling it to neighbouring farmers. The landlords and farmers encourage the practice and the authorities are reluctant to stop it for fear the poor will lose this small source of income. They forget the much larger expense of disease and death which results from this cause.

Stagnant ditches may be seen in the vicinity of most of these houses and part of the ground in the lowest districts is apt to be flooded after heavy rains, and long open sewers cross the public paths. House drains, where they exist, have not been constructed properly and often become choked.

In numerous dwellings a whole family shares one room. But no circumstance has contributed more to the injury of the inhabitants than the tax upon windows.

Three views of the back streets of Newcastle in the 19th century. Why do you think the people in the photograph (left) *look so depressed?* And what do you think is happening in the picture above?

The lodging houses for the extreme poor present the most deplorable examples to be observed in the whole of the city. They are badly crowded, dirty, badly managed, ill-ventilated, where the sexes mix without control. They are generally favoured by the vagrants and trampers, many without employment, and act as nurseries for immorality as well as being a danger to public health. In one there was neither windows nor fireplace. On entering the lodging house, the occupants were attempting to remove a woman who had been attacked with fever. She was most reluctant to leave without all her clothing, which I was told afterwards had been pawned.

The most intolerable nuisance is certainly one resulting from a slaughter-house situated in the very centre just off the most fashionable part of the town. It is close to Grey Street: the nuisance consists in the presence of great quantities of animal matter, the offal of beasts heaped up in an ash-pit. There it is left to rot until liquid streams run down High Friar Lane and fill the neighbourhood with a fearful odour.... Dense black clouds of smoke from manufacturing prevail to great extent in Newcastle and Gateshead. In the lower parts of the town the amount of black smoke is extremely great and their position renders it prone to retain it and other offensive smells. As much as 20 to 50 tons of acid are discharged into the atmosphere.

Water Co.	Source of water	Type of water	Number of water taps	No. of houses	Houses supplied	Price P.A.
Newcastle Joint Stock Company	River Tyne Carr's Hill Cox's Lodge Town Moor Rain water	soft brackish miry hard sooty	20 public	15 000	1 350	18s. to 30s.

Dr D.B. Reid: *Report on the Sanitary Conditions of Newcastle, Gateshead, North Shields, Sunderland, Durham and Carlisle*, 1845

Using the evidence

As an established local doctor, you have been instructed by the Corporation of Newcastle upon Tyne to investigate public health conditions in the city. Using Dr Reid's description, write a report for the Corporation and then make your recommendations at the end. The following headings should be included in your report: Streets and houses; Refuse; Overcrowding; Lodging houses; Slaughter houses; Pollution; Water supply.

THE PROBLEM OF PUBLIC HEALTH

Just imagine for one moment having to live in a street that resembled a stinking open sewer; a place where in summer the smell was unbearable and in winter oozing streams of slime slithered their way into the cellars of houses where the poorest families lived. It is little wonder that many of the people, forced to live in such cramped and dirty conditions, felt that disease could almost be touched in the rotten air they breathed. Death was no stranger to such people. Edwin Chadwick, a campaigner for better sanitary conditions, calculated the average age of death in 1842:

Type of people	Leeds (Town area)	Rutlandshire (Country area)
1. Professional persons, gentry & their families	44 years	52 years
2. Farmers, tradesmen and their families	27 years	41 years
3. Mechanics, labourers and their families	19 years	38 years

Question
Which group of people was most likely to die early?

Your recommendations to the Newcastle Corporation should have given you a clear idea of the problems facing fast-growing industrial towns such as Manchester and Leeds in the nineteenth century. It seems obvious to us (as it did to some people then) that a clean town is a healthy one. Yet little was done to sweep away the conditions described by Dr Reid – conditions which produced the frightening statistics in the table above. Despite the terrible conditions, however, the population increased and large numbers of people were attracted to the towns in the nineteenth century.

Using the evidence

A Population increase

The population of England and Wales 1701–1901			
Year	Population	Year	Population
1701	5.5 millions	1821	12.0 millions
1721	5.8 "	1841	15.9 "
1741	6.0 "	1861	20.1 "
1761	6.7 "	1881	26.0 "
1781	7.9 "	1901	37.0 "
1801	9.5 "		

Questions

1 Before 1801 there was no census (official count of the population) and, therefore, we cannot be absolutely certain how many people were alive at a particular time. Can you think of any ways in which historians might make an intelligent guess about the size of population before 1801?
2 Using the figures from the table, draw a graph showing the change in population 1701–1901.
3 Describe briefly what happened to the size of the population between 1701 and 1901.
4 During which 20-year period did the biggest increase take place?

B Population distribution
The following table shows the percentage of people living a) in the country, and b) in the towns between 1801 and 1881.

Percentage of total population		
Year	Country	Town
1801	69%	31%
1841	54%	46%
1881	32%	68%

Questions

1 Draw two graphs showing the increase in town population and the decrease in countryside population 1801–81.
2 What happened to the distribution of population between 1701 and 1901?

The living conditions left behind in the countryside, however, were no better. Cottages were cold, draughty and crawling with all sorts of vermin. People were not leaving pleasant living conditions when they moved from the countryside to the towns. Bad housing and poor health had always existed; they did not appear just because towns grew.

> It is not many years ago that the cottages had no flooring . . . and that one of lime and sand was held as a luxury. The mud walls were rarely covered with any coat of plastering; there was no ceiling under the straw roof, and when any chamber was in the house it was accessible only by a ladder or by a post with notches indented to receive the foot in climbing to it.
>
> *Quarterly Review*, 1825

C The rate of increase

However, the size and speed of town growth made matters worse. In some cases, towns were totally new, for example Barrow-in-Furness or Crewe. Others, such as Manchester and Birmingham, were established communities which expanded rapidly.

In all these towns more and more people were needing somewhere to live.

A new town: Middlesbrough	
Year	Population
1801	25
1831	154
1841	5 463
1851	7 431
1861	19 416
1871	39 563
1881	55 934
1891	75 532
1901	91 302

An old town: Leeds	
Year	Population
1801	53 162
1811	62 534
1821	83 796
1831	123 393
1841	152 054
1851	171 805

Questions
1 Draw two block graphs showing the growth of each town.
2 Compare the patterns of growth. What differences do you notice?
3 What is the main difference in the timing of rapid expansion?

The Industrial Revolution

Why did these changes take place? The illustrations below give us a clue. What are the differences between the two pictures?

In the late eighteenth and early nineteenth centuries Britain experienced changes which were to alter, for all time, not only the way things were made but also the way we live. These changes are known as the Industrial Revolution. Before this, most manufactured goods were made in workers' homes or small craft workshops in towns. With the invention of machinery such as steam engines and power looms manufacture was concentrated in one building, such as a mill or a factory. This meant that workers had to live close by:

Families were attracted from all parts for the benefit of employment and obliged as a temporary resort to crowd together into such dwellings as the neighbourhood afforded: often two families into one house; others into cellars or very small dwellings; eventually, as the works became established, either the proprietor or some neighbour would probably see it advantageous to build a few cottages; these were often of the worst description; in such cases the prevailing consideration was not how to promote the health and comfort of the occupants, but how many cottages could be built upon the smallest space of ground and at the least possible cost.

Report on the Sanitary Condition of the Labouring Population:
Lords Sessional Report, 1842

An increasing number of people moved to towns and were forced to accept conditions which would not be tolerated today. Most workers earned low wages, particularly in jobs where little skill was necessary, and they could not afford high rents. As a result, houses had to be erected as cheaply as possible. Built back to back, with inferior materials, they looked like rows of barracks. Sometimes they were so poorly built that they fell down. This type of housing was described as 'jerry-built', which means insubstantial.

This poor family's cellar home was typical of the conditions that the workers had to endure. Who do you think the man in the top hat might be?

Some greedy builders 'threw together' buildings to make quick, overnight profits. Others had little money and did not see it as their job to lay sewers or to pipe in fresh water. New housing was not always available and workers found themselves living in overcrowded old houses which had seen better days and did not have adequate water and drainage facilities.

One of the fastest growing cities was Manchester, which grew from a small village in 1700 to be the centre of the cotton industry in 1800. Its population increased three times between 1773 and 1801. Much of the work offered by the mills was unskilled and meant that women and children could be employed. Child labour was not a new idea in itself, but the long hours of work, combined with overcrowded, unhygienic living conditions, made children much more likely victims of injury and disease. The picture presented by the available evidence is not always the same. The following extracts demonstrate this point:

refuse and offal: rubbish and animal remains

Passing along a rough bank, among stakes and washing lines, one penetrates into . . . one storied huts, in most of which there is no proper floor; kitchen, living and sleeping room all in one. In such a hole, scarcely five feet long by six broad, I found two beds . . . a staircase and chimney-place, exactly filled the room. In several others I found absolutely nothing, while the door stood open. . . . Everywhere before the doors refuse and offal [lay;] that any sort of pavement lay underneath could not be seen but only felt, here and there, with the

Above: *cheaply built back-to-back houses were quickly erected in the cities.*
Right: *mills belching smoke in the middle of Manchester*

feet. This whole collection of cattle sheds for human beings was surrounded on two sides by houses and a factory, and on the third by the river....

F. Engels: *The Conditions of the Working Class*, 1844

Questions
1   Engels was a revolutionary who wished to get rid of the factory owners. Why might this make you suspicious of his evidence?
2   Pick out several words or phrases used by Engels to influence the reader.

Andrew Ure, a qualified doctor, also wrote about conditions in Manchester. He described factory children as 'lively little elves' whose work 'seemed to resemble a sport'. He wrote on workers' housing:

commodious: roomy

> *The houses occupied by Mr T. Ashton's work people lie in streets, all built of stone, and are commodious; consisting each of at least four apartments in two stories, with a small backyard and a mews lane. I looked into several of the houses, and found them more richly furnished than any common workpeople's dwellings which I had ever seen before.*

Andrew Ure: *The Philosophy of Manufacturers*, 1835

Questions
1   How does Ure try to convince people that he knows the truth about workers' housing?
2   How does he create a pleasant picture of the conditions, and why would a reader be likely to believe him?
3   What has he not described about the housing which would be a better indication of its sanitary condition?
4   Contrast the two sources. Does one contain lies? Why are they both valuable to an historian?

As you can see, not all writers living in the first half of the nineteenth century present the same picture, which shows us that attitudes to the effects of rapid town growth differed. Both men were writing about the same town. Our reaction is probably to wonder why something was not done to remedy the whole problem of overcrowding, dirt, lack of sanitation and disease. But today we take it for granted that the government is interested in such matters. This was not necessarily the case then, as the next chapter will show.

3 WHY DIDN'T THE GOVERNMENT ACT?

'It's a free country!' is something which you have probably heard often. However, if you think carefully, you will realise that no one is completely free. How free are you? Many laws affect you, but there is one in particular which concerns you until you reach the age of 16. Can you think what law that is?

The law states that you must attend school full time; if you are absent often, without good reason, your parents could be prosecuted and fined. At the same time the local council must, by law, provide schools for the children who live in the area. You *must* attend school; the local education authority *must* provide schools.

Everyone throughout the country must obey the law and the whole of the education service is looked after by the government. Sometimes this is called State Education. 'State' is just another word for 'government'.

Questions
1 a) List three ways you can think of in which the law restricts your freedom.
   b) Try to write against each one the reason why the law limits that particular freedom.
2 List six ways in which the law does not restrict your freedom.
3 Can you think of any laws which in fact increase your freedom as a whole? For example, freedom of speech.

Education is just one part of our everyday life which is controlled by the State, either through the national government or local councils. The list of controls is a long one. Many of these laws are concerned with keeping our environment clean and healthy.

Questions
1 How do local councils try to keep our environment clean and healthy?
2 All these public health services cost a lot of money. How do governments and local councils raise this money?

The examples you have given are a few from the long list of laws and regulations which affect all our lives and are the responsibility of the State. Acts of Parliament are passed and become laws, which we call legislation. Most of them are for our protection. Without drains, water provision, sewerage and health regulations governing how shopkeepers sell goods, or the way in which houses are built, our health would be at risk.

You may already have been wondering why people had to live in the dreadful conditions described at the beginning of this book. Why didn't the government or the local council do something about it? The answer is quite simple. At the beginning of the nineteenth century people had a completely different idea about government and did not expect it to pass laws to control the lives of the people. The fears of people living at the time are well expressed by Thomas Babington Macaulay, a politician and writer. He attacks the idea that government ought to be:

> jack-of-all-trades – architect, engineer, schoolmaster, merchant … a
> Lady Bountiful in every parish, a Paul Pry in every house, spying,
> eavesdropping … spending our money for us, and choosing our
> opinions for us.

T.B. Macaulay: *Critical Essays*, 1829

Thomas Babington Macaulay (1800–59)
Thomas Babington Macaulay entered Parliament when he was 30 years old and came to be regarded as a great speaker. Throughout his career in Parliament, which lasted until 1853, he was interested in matters of social welfare. He was sometimes criticised for being too confident about everything he said or wrote. He belonged to the Whig or Liberal Party.

Edmund Burke (1729–97)
Edmund Burke entered politics at the age of 36. He had several jobs in the Whig Party and supported many causes involving the freedom of individuals and countries. However, he was horrified at the bloodshed of the French Revolution. As a protest he joined the Tory Party and wrote many articles against the Revolution in France.

Thomas Carlyle (1795–1881)
Thomas Carlyle came from a working-class family and was brought up according to strict religious principles. He saw himself as a prophet warning the ruling classes that if they did not accept that they had a responsibility to care for the poor, disaster would follow. He wrote many books denouncing the greed of the society he lived in.

1 Compare this extract with the biographical notes on Macaulay. Does anything strike you as somewhat surprising? Give reasons for your answer.
2 Explain what Macaulay means by the phrases 'Lady Bountiful' and 'Paul Pry'.
3 What jobs does Macaulay fear that the government will take over?
4 What two reasons does Macaulay give for being afraid of increasing the power of the government?

What then did people in the early nineteenth century believe government should be responsible for? The politician Edmund Burke wrote:

magistracy: law and order

> ... *the State ought to confine itself to what regards the State ... namely its magistracy; its revenue; its military force by sea and land ... in a word ... to the public peace, to the public safety, to the public order, to the public prosperity....*
>
> E. Burke: *Thoughts on Security*, 1795

Questions
1 Look at the biographical notes on Edmund Burke. Why do you think he called his book *Thoughts on Security?*
2 Which aspects of the country's life did Burke think the State ought to take into its care?
3 What, therefore, did Burke think the State could not do anything about very effectively?

The attitudes of Macaulay and Burke were typical of the people in power. But as the nineteenth century wore on, more and more people began to say that the State should deal with the problems created by factories, the expansion of towns and the spread of epidemic diseases. Eventually the government had to act; it passed laws to deal with matters which were too big and complicated for individuals to cope with on their own. At first the government acted with great unwillingness.

Although today we find it amazing that it took so long for the government to act, for the people of the time it was a totally new idea which seriously worried them. They were afraid of many things from the cost of providing new services to the damage the government might do to personal freedom. However, writers such as Edwin Chadwick and Thomas Carlyle helped to persuade people to accept that government action was needed:

17

Southwarks, St. Giles's:
London slum areas

wholesome: healthy

Interference has begun; it must continue, must enlarge itself, deepen and sharpen itself . . . . are not Sanitary regulations possible for a Legislature? The old Romans . . . would, I think . . . have rigorously seen rammed up into total abolition many a foul cellar in our Southwarks, St. Giles's, and dark poison lanes, saying starkly, 'Shall a Roman dwell there?' The Legislature, even as it now is, could order all dingy Manufacturing Towns to cease from their soot and darkness; to let in the blessed sunlight, the blue of heaven and become clear and clean . . . . Baths, free air, a wholesome temperature, ceilings twenty feet high, might be ordained, by Act of Parliament, in all establishments licensed as mills . . . . A willing Legislature could say so with effect and would answer 'Yes . . . my sons and daughters will gain health, and life, and a soul.'

Thomas Carlyle: *Past and Present*, 1843

Questions
1 Why do you think Thomas Carlyle states that the Romans would have abolished the slum areas of Southwark and St Giles?
2 Give two examples of laws which Carlyle wanted the government to pass.
3 Give two examples of the benefits which Carlyle thought would result from government action.

A cartoon from Punch, *attacking the unhygienic living conditions of the poor in the 19th century*

It was, however, terrifying diseases such as cholera which shocked the government into action. In the next chapter you will read about the effects of this disease when it struck in 1831.

THE 1832 CHOLERA EPIDEMIC

The nineteenth century doctor: kill or cure?

British doctors in the late eighteenth and early nineteenth century had fairly limited knowledge of disease and illness by comparison with present-day doctors. Their training was not very extensive, particularly if they lived outside London, and they did not have to go to medical school or university. Instead, they served an apprenticeship with a recognised medical practitioner.

These doctors' ideas about illness and disease were based on a curious mixture of ancient Greek beliefs (for example, that the body contained fluids which had to be kept in balance), common sense remedies based on centuries of trial and error, a very basic knowledge of anatomy and, finally, some mistaken theories. Very often the doctors depended on an apothecary for their drugs or for information on how to prepare medicine. An apothecary was the nearest example of what we call a chemist. He would often give medical advice to the poor who could not afford the fees of a physician. The very poor, however, relied on traditional and often useless cures, such as eating young frogs to cure asthma.

Although Hogarth's Anatomy Lesson *dates from 1751, knowledge spread slowly and few 19th century doctors understood much about the body's internal organs*

Treatments were sometimes worse than the illness. Bleeding, either by opening a vein or by applying leeches, was a favourite remedy. Blistering areas of the body, giving laxatives, laudanum (opium) or mixtures that caused the patient to vomit, were all standard treatments.

Most important of all, although doctors were aware of germs, they believed them to be the result of disease. It was not until the later years of the nineteenth century that doctors generally accepted germs to be the cause of disease. So, the conditions in which disease thrives were not improved. It was thought that disease travelled in bad air, a 'poisonous miasma', as it was called. Doctors were aware that disease could be spread through contact, but they did not know exactly how the process worked.

This brief summary of the condition of medicine shows how badly equipped the doctors were and explains how difficult it was for the local physician to cope with epidemics such as cholera. Any doctor who was able to suggest ways of dealing with the disease, perhaps because he had come across it abroad, was often regarded with suspicion by other doctors or with disbelief by people in positions of authority. After all, doctors were not held in the highest trust, which is understandable in view of the information above.

Cholera's journey

Rumours began to reach England early in 1818 of an outbreak of cholera in India. Cholera is a highly infectious disease which attacks the intestines and causes violent diarrhoea and sickness, cramp, fever and death. This epidemic seems to have begun in August 1817 in Jessore (112 kilometres from Calcutta); it died down during the winter and then burst out with renewed force in the spring of 1818. Not only did the disease travel across India, it also spread beyond its frontiers.

Questions
1 Copy the map of cholera's journey into your book, marking on it the main rivers, cities and mountain ranges, the route of the epidemic and the dates of its arrival.
2 Look at the features of the map and write an explanation of why the epidemic spread from port to port and major city to major city.
3 Read the information around the map.
    a) What evidence is there that people panicked?
    b) What sensible measures were taken in some places?
    c) What evidence is there that some people took advantage of panic?

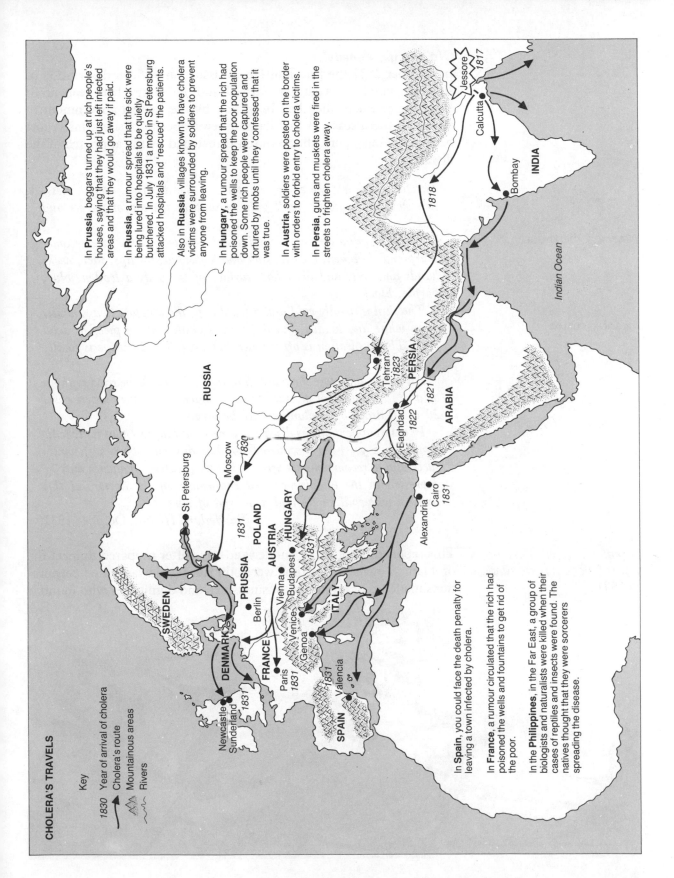

CHOLERA'S TRAVELS

Key

1830 Year of arrival of cholera

  Cholera's route

  Mountainous areas

  Rivers

In **Prussia**, beggars turned up at rich people's houses, saying that they had just left infected areas and that they would go away if paid.

In **Russia**, a rumour spread that the sick were being lured into hospitals to be quietly butchered. In July 1831 a mob in St Petersburg attacked hospitals and 'rescued' the patients.

Also in **Russia**, villages known to have cholera victims were surrounded by soldiers to prevent anyone from leaving.

In **Hungary**, a rumour spread that the rich had poisoned the wells to keep the poor population down. Some rich people were captured and tortured by mobs until they 'confessed' that it was true.

In **Austria**, soldiers were posted on the border with orders to forbid entry to cholera victims.

In **Persia**, guns and muskets were fired in the streets to frighten cholera away.

In **Spain**, you could face the death penalty for leaving a town infected by cholera.

In **France**, a rumour circulated that the rich had poisoned the wells and fountains to get rid of the poor.

In the **Philippines**, in the Far East, a group of biologists and naturalists were killed when their cases of reptiles and insects were found. The natives thought that they were sorcerers spreading the disease.

Jessore *1817*

Calcutta

1818

Bombay

INDIA

Indian Ocean

RUSSIA

Tehran *1823*

PERSIA

1821

Baghdad *1822*

ARABIA

Cairo *1831*

Alexandria

St Petersburg

Moscow

1830

POLAND

1831

PRUSSIA

Berlin

AUSTRIA

Vienna

HUNGARY

Budapest *1831*

SWEDEN

DENMARK

1831

FRANCE

Paris *1831*

Venice

Genoa

ITALY

1831

Valencia

SPAIN

Newcastle

Sunderland

21

'No specific remedy'

In October 1831 the Board of Health issued an official description of cholera, based on what Dr Russell and Dr Barry had seen at St Petersburg, where they had been sent by the British government to report on the disease. A Sunderland newspaper published this report because, being a port, the town felt threatened by the approach of the disease:

> The following are the early symptoms of the disease . . . giddiness, sick stomach, slow or small pulse, cramp at the top of fingers and toes. . . .
>
> Vomiting or purging of a liquid like rice-water . . . the face becomes sharp and shrunken, the eyes sink and look wild, the lips, face, neck, hands and feet, and the whole surface of the body a leaden, blue, purple, black. . . .
>
> The skin is deadly cold and often damp, the tongue always moist, often white and loaded, but flabby and chilled like a piece of dead flesh. The respiration is often quick but irregular . . . urine is totally stopped.
>
> All means to restore the warmth of the body should be tried without delay . . . poultices of mustard to the stomach . . . in very severe cases 20 to 40 drops of laudanum may be given. . . .
>
> In the treatment of this disease it is necessary to state that no specific remedy has yet been discovered nor has any cure been sufficiently successful to recommend its use . . . but the greatest confidence may be expressed in the intelligence and enthusiasm of the doctors of this country who will surely find a method of cure.
>
> Sunderland Herald, October 1831

purging: diarrhoea

loaded: coated

poultices: pads

This report did not make Sunderland any better prepared to meet the problem. Towns at this time were still run by old-fashioned corporations made up of important businessmen and dignitaries who found it

A sketch of a girl who died from cholera in Sunderland in 1831

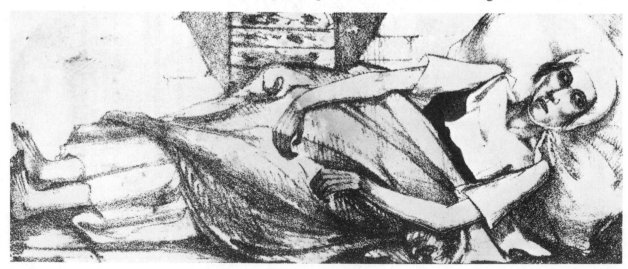

very difficult to manage the new problems posed by growing industry and increasing population. Nevertheless, the Central Board of Health in London gave permission for towns to set up their own local boards to deal with outbreaks of disease. The members of such boards were not always certain of the actions they could take. Some worked hard. Others, however, did little or nothing. The problem can be shown clearly by investigating the spread of cholera in Sunderland and Newcastle in the north east of England.

Questions

1 Why did the *Sunderland Herald* print this report?
2 Imagine you are a doctor in Sunderland in 1831. After reading the report on cholera in the local newspaper, you are called to visit a young girl who has suddenly become ill. Describe first what you would look for when trying to decide if the patient has cholera, and then the treatments that you might try.
3 Why would doctors and patients be worried about the report?
4 How did the Board try to calm people's fears? Why would the government do this?
5 Look at the picture of the girl who died from cholera. How would you recognise that she had died of the disease?

Cholera reaches Sunderland

In the early nineteenth century Sunderland was made up of three separate areas with a total population of about 40 000.

The population of Sunderland town was about 19 000 and was mainly working class. An important group of workers was the closely knit band of keelmen, who ferried coal in keels or barges along the river from the inland collieries to the ocean-going coal ships. Most of

The waterfront, Sunderland

Dr Reid Clanny

the working-class community lived in small, overcrowded houses huddled into narrow lanes or courts, many of which were damp and unhealthy. The two other communities were Monkwearmouth and the small, more prosperous district of Bishopswearmouth, where professional men, businessmen, shipowners, merchants and traders lived.

The amount of the port's trade varied. Sometimes it did well, at other times not so well. It was the home port for 600 ships and had a capacity for 200 ships at any one time.

The Sunderland Board of Health met for the first time in June 1831, under the chairmanship of Mr Robinson, a local magistrate. It was to set up a committee of doctors to advise the Board. One of the doctors would also be a member of the Board. The highly respected Dr Reid Clanny was chosen for this job, having been senior physician to the Sunderland Infirmary. Among those present at the first meeting called by Clanny was an army surgeon, Dr James Kell, who had seen a cholera epidemic in India. Although he could only give advice, he knew people with power and influence.

The first officially recorded case of cholera in Sunderland was William Sproat. Four days after Sproat died, Kell reported the case to Robinson and official action was finally taken. At the same time, Kell informed the Central Board of Health in London that cholera had struck in Sunderland.

Dr Clanny's casebook

Victim 1:

William Sproat, aged sixty years, a keelman, employed at the pier, had been for a week or ten days affected with diarrhoea; but he was not so ill as to be obliged to relinquish his employment. . . . On Wednesday morning, October 19th, he became worse, and was unable to continue his work. On Thursday evening, October 20th, at 6 o'clock I was called to him, and found him vomiting and purging, but with no symptom of collapse.

On Wednesday morning, October 26th, he was much weaker; the pulse scarcely beating under the fingers, countenance quite shrunk, eyes sunk, lips dark blue . . . at twelve o'clock at noon he died. . . .

Victim 2:

I now proceed to the next case. On 27th of October, accompanied by Mr Kell, I visited, by request, William Sproat, son of William Sproat senior. . . . We found him in a low damp cellar, near the Fish Quay, close to the river, and also to his late father's residence. . . .

The attack commenced with copious fluid, tainted with blood. He had been severely purged, and the quantity of rice-like water which passed was immense. The surface of the body was cold.

Victim 3:

Thomas Wilson, keelman, aged 51, a man of regular habits, was

relinquish: give up

countenance: face

copious: plentiful
tainted: stained

regular habits: healthy

24

attacked on the morning of 31st October, about 4 o'clock, with
vomiting of a fluid resembling rice-water. . . . I left him, and saw him
again at 12 o'clock; had the appearance of a living corpse . . . . He
gradually got worse, and expired at 3 o'clock.

Victim 4:

stimulants: drugs

Eliza Turnbull, a strong healthy woman, was one of the nurses at the
Infirmary, was taken ill yesterday morning, October 31st about one
o'clock. . . . A vein was opened in each arm, from which flowed only
a few drops of blood, like treacle. External and internal stimulants
with opium, were freely used, without effect. . . .

It may be necessary to state that she had no other communication
with any person labouring under cholera, than in assisting, the
preceding evening, to remove, from the fever house to the dead house,
the body of a person who had just died of that disease.

alluded to: mentioned

The body here alluded to was that of William Sproat, the second,
whose case is previously recorded.

Dr R. Clanny: *A description of the recent visitation of cholera to*
Sunderland, Gateshead and Newcastle, 1832

Questions

Victims 1 and 2, the Sproats

1   Why was Kell useful in dealing with the outbreak?
2   Can you think of any reason why Sproat would have been a
    likely victim of the disease?
3   How do you think the son might have caught the disease?
4   In what kind of housing conditions did the Sproats live?

Victim 3, Thomas Wilson

5   What was Wilson's job? Could he have been in contact with the
    Sproats?
6   If you had been called to treat Wilson and the others, what
    symptoms would have caused you to diagnose cholera?

Victim 4, Eliza Turnbull

7   What was Eliza's job? Whose body had she helped to remove
    from the fever house?
8   There were two theories about how cholera was passed on.
    The first was the 'miasmic' idea, that disease was carried in foul
    air. The second theory was the 'contagion' idea, that the
    disease was passed on by contact with a cholera victim or the
    victim's clothes or bed linen. Read the case histories of William
    Sproat junior and Eliza Turnbull again. Under two headings,
    Miasmic and Contagion, note down any fact which might be
    used to demonstrate one theory or the other.

Selfish shipowners?

After receiving information from Mr Kell, the government ordered that the port of Sunderland be put into quarantine (no ship was allowed in or out).

Naturally enough, the shipowners disliked the interruption of their trade and interference with their livelihood. A meeting was held at the Royal Exchange, Sunderland, on 11 November, 1831, for shipowners and leading citizens. Certain doctors were asked to deny the fact that cholera had arrived in Sunderland. By doing this they hoped to persuade the government to lift the quarantine order.

Royal Exchange, Sunderland
11th November, 1831

Public meeting of shipowners, merchants and other inhabitants of Sunderland most numerously attended.

Resolved:

unqualified: definite

It is the unqualified opinion of this meeting, based on Parish Inspectors, that this town is now in a more healthy state than is usual for this time of year. We have made extensive enquiries about this disorder which has caused panic throughout the kingdom and we have found it not Indian Cholera. The few deaths of sickness in the last six weeks have been caused through common bowel complaints and is caused through want and uncleanliness.

2nd motion:

The paragraph put in the London papers on the 4th November, stating that Indian Cholera was brought to Sunderland by a Hamburg ship, is a wicked and malicious falsehood. It is our belief that no seaman or Customs Officer of the port has any such complaint.

3rd motion:

transit: carrying

The measures adopted by His Majesty's Government forcing Sunderland ships into quarantine and guarding them by a warship is totally uncalled for especially since the transit of all types of goods on land by transport on coaches is being permitted, through the rest of the country.

5th motion:

ascertaining: making sure

This meeting regrets deeply that any individual saw fit to give such information to H.M. Government without ascertaining it to be a fact and then informing us the Principal Inhabitants and it is to be hoped this practice will not be repeated.

Questions

1 What claims are the Sunderland shipowners and merchants making about the cholera outbreak?

2 What are they contradicting?
3 What activity in the port of Sunderland has the government forbidden?
4 Who is the individual mentioned in the 5th motion?
5 What effects would a quarantine produce on the profits of the coal owners, shipowners and merchants in the town?
6 Why might the workers, who were most likely to catch cholera, also object to the quarantine?
7 Would the shipowners have known for certain that the quarantine would prevent the spread of cholera?
8 In your exercise book, draw up a chart headed 'Selfish shipowners?' Divide the page into two columns. In one column, under the heading 'Evidence for', list information which could be used to show that the shipowners were acting selfishly. In the second column, under the heading 'Evidence against', list information which could be used to show that the shipowners were acting sensibly within the knowledge available to them at that time.

Lord Londonderry's letter

Just as the shipowners were annoyed by the quarantine, so a coal owner would be displeased by the drop in his profits once trade had been halted. Lord Londonderry was the richest and most influential coal owner in the north east of England. He wrote to a London newspaper. On 19 November 1831 a copy of his letter was published by the *Sunderland Herald*, which also printed a copy of a letter from a Dr Brown to Lord Londonderry:

The following letters have been addressed to a London evening paper:–

Seaham Hall, Nov. 13.

Sir,

The enclosed letter ... will ... tranquilize the public mind, as to the appearance of Cholera at Sunderland. As I reside within five miles, I have taken every means to be informed on the subject, and I feel quite satisfied the reports and statements of this fatal malady have been greatly exaggerated. Individual opinions may be lightly treated, but so convinced am I of the fallacy of many of the accounts ... that I shall neither remove my family nor myself from the neighbourhood.... The letter I send is from Dr. Brown, a very old army medical officer, who served with me, and who is now in constant attendance on my family....

Your obedient servant,

Vane Londonderry

Lord Londonderry

fatal malady: deadly illness
fallacy: mistaken belief

My Lord,

... The conclusions to which I have attained, from all I have witnessed are –

1. *That the disease has certainly not been imported.*
2. *That it is not contagious.*
3. *That it has attacked ... the lowest orders, living in the worst situations and ... broken down by previous disease, old age or intemperance.*
4. *That it is very much subsiding.*
5. *That the commercial restrictions are totally superfluous as the disease is not communicable....*

The shipowners and merchants are in a sad uproar ... vessels from here are subject to fifteen days quarantine.

Your Lordship's Obedient Servant

J. Brown

We have only to add, the public mind is naturally much excited; and if anyone dies, and the slightest symptom of cholera has made its appearance in the ... illness, why the inference is immediately made that the death has proceeded from cholera, although as everyone knows, several of the symptoms of cholera are present in many diseases....

intemperance: abuse of body, *i.e.* by drink

communicable: infectious

inference: deduction

Questions

1 What reasons would have prompted Lord Londonderry to write such a letter to the newspaper?
2 How does he attempt to put people's minds at rest?
3 Why has he enclosed the letter from Dr Brown?
4 Can you think of any reasons why Dr Brown would have written this letter for Lord Londonderry?
5 According to the doctor, which people had been attacked by the disease?
6 From your knowledge of the case histories of the Sproats, Thomas Wilson and Eliza Turnbull, which of the doctor's points are correct and which are incorrect?
7 Why might the people of the town be convinced by these letters?
8 Was Lord Londonderry likely to have known the true situation in Sunderland? Give a reason for your answer.

Prevention?

Various institutions and individuals began to respond to, or cash in on, the epidemic. Two extracts from the *Sunderland Herald*, November 1831, illustrate this:

A Aid chemical (an advertisement)

IMPORTANT!!!

At all seasons of the year, but particularly so at the present Period, whilst the Atmosphere is undergoing sudden Changes, generating and increasing infectious disorders, and especially whilst the Public Mind is distracted with Fears lest that dreadful Scourge to Mankind,

THE CHOLERA MORBUS,

should visit this Neighbourhood, it cannot be too generally known that the Ravages of that most formidable Disease may be arrested, and the Progress of Fevers, of the most dangerous and contagious Character, suspended by the free Use of the Concentrated Disinfecting Solutions of

CHLORIDE OF LIME,
& CHLORIDE OF SODA,
of a Uniform Strength,
Prepared with the greatest Exactness, and sold Wholesale and Retail by

JOHN RITSON
CHEMIST AND DRUGGIST,
NO. 4
High Street, Sunderland.

B Aid spiritual (a report)

LONDON, NOV. 7
FORM OF PRAYERS TO BE READ IN
ALL CHURCHES

... His Grace The Archbishop of Canterbury ... adopted the following prayers to be read in all ... Churches ... throughout the Kingdom:—

'Most Gracious Father and God! ... Look down, we beseech thee, from Heaven. ... O Merciful Father, suffer not thy destroying angel to lift up his hand against us, but keep us, as thou hast heretofore done, in health and safety; and grant, that by being warned by the sufferings of others to repent of our sins, we may be preserved from all evil by thy mighty protection, and enjoy the continuance of thy mercy and grace.

Through Jesus Christ.
Amen.'

Questions

1 In the advertisement, what does Ritson claim that his chloride of lime can do?
2 Does he present any evidence to support his claim?
3 What does he think is the cause of the spread of cholera?
4 Why might you distrust this advertisement?
5 Why should Ritson concentrate on cholera in the advertisement?
6 You are a quack doctor who claims to have found a miracle cure for cholera. Draw a poster advertising your cure. Think carefully about how you would attract customers.
7 In the archbishop's prayer, what is thought to be the reason for the cholera outbreak in Britain?
8 In the prayer, how is it suggested that people can escape the disease?
9 How might such prayers help the people faced by the threat of the epidemic at the time?

A political cartoonist's view of the cholera epidemic

10 Look at the cartoon.
   a) What treatments are being attempted?
   b) What is the cartoonist's attitude towards doctors and their cures? Explain your answer carefully.
   c) Why was the cartoonist's attitude likely to have been a common one at that time?

CLAIMED BY KING CHOLERA

The cholera epidemic rapidly became more serious, forcing the government to take strong action. This consisted of issuing orders about the burial of the dead and disposal of corpses not less than six feet underground.

A

NOTICE.

Durham,
to wit.

WE, the undersigned Magistrates, acting for the Town of Sunderland, in the said County, do, in virtue of the powers vested in us, by a Proclamation issued by a Committee of the Lords of His Majesty's Most Honourable Privy Council, and dated the 11th of November 1831, and at the suggestion and advice of the Board, at present constituted for the Preservation of the Health of the Inhabitants of the said Town, hereby promulgate the following Orders and Regulations, that is to say,—

"That all Persons dying of Cholera, be buried within Twelve Hours after their decease, at latest; and that their Graves be dug not less than of the depth of Six Feet, if possible, and in Ground to be set apart and appropriated for that purpose only."

And we, the said Magistrates, do hereby enjoin and require all Persons strictly to obey and attend to the foregoing Orders and Regulations; and do also warn and admonish them, that, in case of any disobedience thereto, they will incur all the Pains and Penalties mentioned and referred to in and by the said Proclamation.

A. FENWICK.
T. WILKINSON.
J. D. GARTHWAITE.

Sunderland,
9th December, 1831.

constituted: set up
promulgate: issue

appropriated: used

enjoin: command

incur: receive

A public notice setting out the new burial regulations, 1831

B *Nearly the whole of the labouring population . . . (dock labourers, navigators, brick-layers' labourers) . . . have only one room. The corpse is therefore kept in that room where the inmates sleep and have their meals. Sometimes the corpse is stretched on the bed, and the bed and bedclothes taken off, and the wife and family lie on the floor. Sometimes a board is got on which the corpse is stretched, and that is sustained on tressels or on chairs. Sometimes it is stretched on two chairs. When children die, they are frequently laid out on the table. The poor Irish, if they can afford it, form a canopy of white calico over the corpse. . . .*

The time the corpse is kept varies according to the day of the death. . . . Bodies are almost always kept for a full week, frequently longer. . . .

E. Chadwick:
Report into the Practice of Interment in Towns, 1843

C *Ordered that the unclaimed bodies of paupers dying in the Workhouse be delivered to the School of Anatomy now held in the Surgeons Hall in this town pursuant to the Act of Parliament in that case made. . . .*

pursuant: following

Minutes of the Newcastle Workhouse, *circa* 1840

Questions

1 In view of the notice about burial regulations, do you think Lord Londonderry's letter was successful in persuading the authorities that the cholera epidemic was no more than a scare? Give a reason for your answer.
2 Read the extract from Chadwick's report, then write down reasons why magistrates would find it necessary to issue burial rules.
3 For what reasons would unclaimed pauper bodies be delivered to the School of Anatomy?

All Saints Church, Newcastle

Burying the victims

Despite all the regulations, cholera spread from Sunderland to nearby towns. Newcastle, the business centre of the north east of England, eventually fell victim to the disease. The parish of All Saints in Newcastle was made up of warehouses and overcrowded slums known as the Sandgate. The list of burials reveals many aspects of life in the 1830s, but in particular it tells us about cholera's death toll.

Name	Abode	When Buried	Age	By Whom Ceremony Performed	
1831					
John Graham Fenwick	Walker	Dec. 2 Fri.	9 weeks	W.A. Shute	
Jane Bell	Pointer Heugh	Dec. 5	79 yrs.	" "	
Elizabeth Miller	Sandgate	Dec. 4	17 yrs.	" "	
Elizabeth Hedley	Butcher Bank	Dec. 4	61 yrs.	" "	
Joseph Miller	Side	Dec. 5	9 days	" "	
Richard Cooper	Sandgate	Dec. 7	1½ yrs.	" "	
Mary Marchbank	Sandgate	Dec. 9 Fri.	75 yrs.	" "	Cholera
Ann Dixon	Sandgate	Dec. 9	27 yrs.	" "	
Elizabeth Richardson	New Road	Dec. 10	77 yrs.	" "	Cholera
Jane Cadwallader	New Pandon St	Dec. 11	13 yrs.	" "	
Isaac Wailes	Sandgate	Dec. 12	23 yrs.	" "	Cholera
Margaret Dodds	Silver St	Dec. 12	11 yrs.	" "	
Helen McDonald	Sandgate	Dec. 12	25 yrs.	" "	Cholera
Isabella Pybus	Poor's House	Dec. 13	91 yrs.	" "	
James Robson	Eldon Place	Dec. 13	14 days	" "	
William Clark	Low Bridge	Dec. 13	40 yrs.	" "	
Elizabeth Ridley	New Pandon St	Dec. 13	70 yrs.	" "	Cholera
Ann Carrick	Pilgrim St	Dec. 15	50 yrs.	" "	
Grace Leonard	Sandgate	Dec. 15	6 yrs.	" "	Cholera
Ann Clarke	Sandgate	Dec. 15	35 yrs.	" "	Cholera
Jane Scott	Pandon	Dec. 15	54 yrs.	" "	Cholera
John Ridley	New Pandon St	Dec. 15	39 yrs.	" "	Cholera
Thomas Ridley	New Pandon St	Dec. 15	2½ yrs.	" "	Cholera
Isabella Hidley	Sandgate	Dec. 16 Fri.	35 yrs.	" "	Cholera
Elizabeth Mewing (?)	Trafalgar St	Dec. 17	58 yrs.	" "	Cholera
Peter Leonard	Sandgate	Dec. 17	3 yrs.	" "	Cholera
Mary Jackson	Trinity House	Dec. 18	85 yrs.	" "	
Ann Donnison	North Shore	Dec. 18	25 yrs.		Suspicious
William Smith	Sandgate	Dec. 19	72 yrs.	" "	
Mary Smith	Sandgate	Dec. 20	45 yrs.	" "	Cholera
Elizabeth Walker	Sandgate	Dec. 21	–	M. Plummer	Cholera
Ann Anderson	Sandgate	Dec. 21	47 yrs.	" "	Cholera
(?) Hanncell Dantze	Lunatic Asylum, West Gate	Dec. 21	–	" "	
James Thompson	Sandgate	Dec. 22	–	W.A. Shute	Cholera
Mary Muffatee	Sandgate	Dec. 22	36 yrs.	" "	Cholera
Thomas Jolling	North Shore	Dec. 22	28 yrs.	I. Manisty	Cholera
Elizabeth Clint	North Shore	Dec. 23 Fri.	50 yrs.	W.A. Shute	Cholera
Ann Wailes	North Shore	Dec. 23	35 yrs.	" "	Cholera
Mary Charlton	Sandgate	Dec. 23	2 weeks	" "	
William McLaughlin	Sandgate	Dec. 23	70 yrs.	" "	Cholera
Elizabeth McConnic	Sandgate	Dec. 24	5 yrs.	" "	
Elizabeth Richardson	Sandgate	Dec. 24	22 yrs.	" "	Cholera
Ann Wilkinson	Pandon Bank	Dec. 24	49 yrs.	Robt. Greek	Cholera
Esther Smith	Sandgate	Dec. 25	40 yrs.	" "	Cholera
Jane Davison	Sandgate	Dec. 25	45 yrs.	" "	Cholera
Ann Orrick	Nelson St	Dec. 25	31 yrs.	W.A. Shute	
Winifred Hines	Sandgate	Dec. 26	67 yrs.	" "	

Name	Abode	When Buried	Age	By Whom Ceremony Performed	
Elizabeth Mooney	Sandgate	Dec. 26	75 yrs.	W.A. Shute	
Robert Dickinson	High Bridge	Dec. 26	35 yrs.	" "	Cholera
Jane Bell	Hospital	Dec. 27	72 yrs.	" "	Cholera
Margaret Forsyth	Mount Pleasant	Dec. 28	11 yrs.	" "	Cholera
George Pinkerton	Broad Chare	Dec. 28	85 yrs.	" "	Cholera
Isabella Peacock	Clarence Place	Dec. 28	56 yrs.	" "	Cholera
Martha Elliott	Blue Anchor Chare	Dec. 28	40 yrs.	" "	Cholera
Ann Sloan	New Pandon St	Dec. 29	45 yrs.	" "	Cholera
Mary Ann Jones	Black Row	Dec. 29	14 yrs.	" "	Cholera
Elizabeth Hunter	Low Bridge	Dec. 29	36 yrs.	" "	Cholera
Peter Keevins	Wall Knolls	Dec. 29	28 yrs.	" "	Cholera
Richard Urwin	Pilgrim St	Dec. 30 Fri.	40 yrs.	" "	Cholera
Mary Dixon	Silver St	Dec. 30	48 yrs.	" "	Cholera
Elizabeth Heslop	Sandgate	Dec. 30	78 yrs.	" "	Suspicious
Elizabeth Young	Silver St	Dec. 30	26 yrs.	" "	Cholera
Eleanor Laslie	Manor Chare	Dec. 31	50 yrs.	" "	Cholera
Elizabeth Watson	Stock Bridge	Dec. 31	10 month	" "	Cholera
Mary Noble	Prudhoe	Dec. 31	34 yrs.	" "	Cholera
Jane Summerbell	Butcher Bank	Dec. 31	65 yrs.	" "	Cholera

1832

Name	Abode	When Buried	Age	By Whom Ceremony Performed	
Elizabeth Blackbird	Wall Knolls	Jan. 2	54 yrs.	Robt. Greek	Cholera
John Loftus	Postern	Jan. 2	$1\frac{3}{4}$ yrs.	W.A. Shute	Cholera
Sarah Alnwick	St Peters	Jan. 2	73 yrs.	" "	Cholera
Mary Steel	Ouseburn	Jan. 2	85 yrs.	I. Manisty	Cholera
William Bauhuer	Poor's House	Jan. 3	30 yrs.	W.A. Shute	Suspicious
Robert Dixon	Castle Garth	Jan. 4	70 yrs.	" "	Cholera
Jane Ellison	Sandgate	Jan. 5	32 yrs.	" "	Cholera
Eleanor Douglas	Sandgate	Jan. 5	50 yrs.	" "	Cholera
Elizabeth McGraw	Pilgrim St	Jan. 6 Fri.	4 yrs.	" "	
George Burrell	Peut's Hole	Jan. 8	$4\frac{1}{2}$ yrs.	Robt. Greek	
Ottoway Reed	Peut's Hole	Jan. 8	$4\frac{1}{2}$ yrs.	" "	
William Elliott	Bewcastle Chare	Jan. 8	1 yr.	" "	
Mary Rutter	St Anne's Row	Jan. 8	81 yrs.	W.A. Shute	
John Dixon	Ballest Hills	Jan. 8	61 yrs.	" "	Cholera
Ann Henwright	Newgate St	Jan. 10	75 yrs.	" "	
James Turnbull	Quay	Jan. 10	3 mths.	" "	
Simon Armstrong	Carliol St	Jan. 10	28 yrs.	" "	
Euphemia Burrell	Bewcastle Chare	Jan. 10	53 yrs.	" "	Cholera
Mary Oliver	Gallowgate	Jan. 10	70 yrs.	" "	Suspicious
Andrew Reay	Keelmens' Hosp.	Jan. 11	61 yrs.	" "	Cholera
George Nevins	North Shore	Jan. 11	57 yrs.	" "	
Michael Carter	New Road	Jan. 12	$1\frac{1}{2}$ yrs.	" "	Cholera
John Thompson	Poor's House	Jan. 13 Fri.	70 yrs.	" "	Suspicious
George Jobling	Walker	Jan. 13	25 yrs.	" "	Cholera
William Blenkinsopp	Dog Bank	Jan. 15	4 yrs.	I. Manisty	
John Bioun	Stock Bridge	Jan. 15	52 yrs.	" "	Cholera

Name	Abode	When Buried	Age	By Whom Ceremony Performed	
Ann Smith	Forth St	Jan. 16	9 mths.	" "	
Jane Colewell	Middle St	Jan. 16	30 yrs.	" "	Cholera
Mary Jones	Back Row	Jan. 16	39 yrs.	" "	Cholera
Elizabeth Wilson	George's Stairs	Jan. 16	61 yrs.	" "	Cholera
Mary Robottom	Middle St	Jan. 17	76 yrs.	W.A. Shute	Cholera
John Cummings	Craigs Alley	Jan. 17	9 yrs.	" "	Cholera
Mary Nicholson	Dog Bank	Jan. 17	24 yrs.	" "	
Penelope Hughses	Sandgate	Jan. 17	54 yrs.	" "	Cholera
Elizabeth Bissett	Close	Jan. 17	81 yrs.	" "	Cholera
James McCormack	Heath's Entry	Jan. 18	5 yrs.	" "	Cholera
Dorothy Buston	Ouseburn	Jan. 18	39 yrs.	" "	Cholera
Mary Hudson	St Lawrence	Jan. 18	$1\frac{1}{2}$ yrs.	" "	Cholera
Mary Broadbert	Byker	Jan. 19	29 yrs.	" "	Cholera
Mary Blackey	Wall Knoll	Jan. 19	42 yrs.	" "	Cholera
Jane Wright	Silver St	Jan. 20 Fri.	81 yrs.	" "	Cholera
Nicholas Giles	New Road	Jan. 20	68 yrs.	" "	Cholera
Frances Moore	High Bridge	Jan. 20	69 yrs.	" "	
Isabella Robson	North Shore	Jan. 20	22 yrs.	" "	Cholera
William Charlton	Sandgate	Jan. 20	9 wks.	" "	
Martha Forster	Gateshead	Jan. 20	36 yrs.	" "	Cholera
Catherine Percy	Glass House	Jan. 21	42 yrs.	" "	Cholera
John Harley	Sandgate	Jan. 21	$1\frac{1}{2}$ yrs.	" "	Cholera
Mary Mosman	Stock Bridge	Jan. 22	85 yrs.	" "	
Ann Rutherford	North Shore	Jan. 22	80 yrs.	" "	
Catherine Dhu	Stock Bridge	Jan. 22	–	" "	Suspected
Joseph Fell	Pilgrim St	Jan. 23	60 yrs.	Rob. Greek	
Stephen Dixon	Pandon Bank	Jan. 23	53 yrs.	W.A. Shute	Cholera
Joseph Percy	Glass House	Jan. 25	1 wk.	" "	Cholera
Isabella Percy	St Anthony's	Jan. 27 Fri.	67 yrs.	" "	

Register of deaths, All Saints parish, Newcastle upon Tyne

Questions

1 Why would some deaths be regarded as suspicious?

2 Would you count suspicious deaths with those from cholera?

3 Plot on a bar graph the total number of deaths week by week as recorded in the Parish Register. Plot under the first column graph the number of cholera deaths per week. In which week did most deaths from cholera occur?

4 Plot the number of deaths according to age, i.e. 0–10, 11–20 and so on, on a bar graph. The majority of history books tell us that the highest mortality rate was among infants. Do the results of your graph confirm this view?

5 Some victims' ages are not recorded in the register. Why do you think this might be?

6 What else does the Parish Register reveal about life in the 1830s?

Street by street

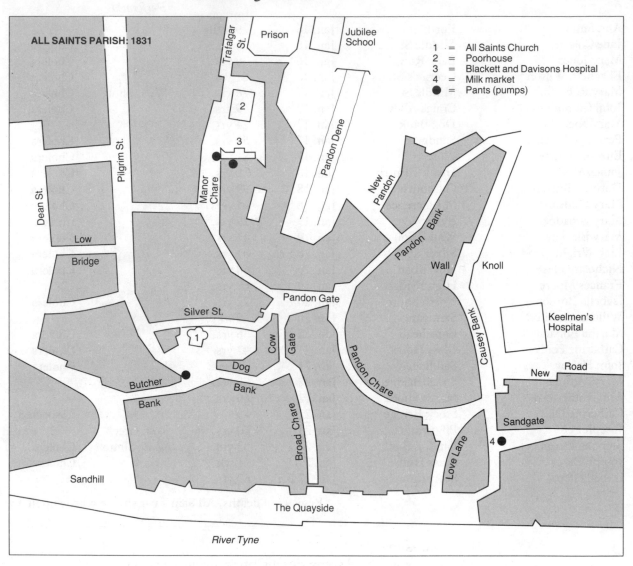

ALL SAINTS PARISH: 1831

1 = All Saints Church
2 = Poorhouse
3 = Blackett and Davisons Hospital
4 = Milk market
● = Pants (pumps)

Prison

Jubilee School

Trafalgar St.

Pandon Dene

New Pandon

Pandon Bank

Wall

Knoll

Keelmen's Hospital

Pilgrim St.

Dean St.

Low

Bridge

Manor Chare

Pandon Gate

Silver St.

Cow

Gate

Pandon Chare

Causey Bank

New Road

Butcher

Dog

Bank

Bank

Broad Chare

Sandgate

Sandhill

Love Lane

4

The Quayside

River Tyne

Questions

1 Make a list of the streets in All Saints parish in which cholera deaths were recorded.
2 Beside each street on your list mark down the number of cholera deaths which occurred there.
3 Trace the map into your book. Using different colours, shade in those streets which suffered one, two, three, four, five, six to 20, or more than 20 deaths.
4 Look at your map again and try to pinpoint the places which provided those streets with an essential item or service and which might have been cholera breeding grounds.

The scourge spreads

No regulation could stop the sinister spread of the disease. People no longer asked whether it would come. Instead, they asked when it would arrive. By the end of January 1832 cholera reached Edinburgh; Glasgow was infected by early February. Within 18 months 10 000 Scots lay rotting in the earth, and two-thirds of that number were from the two large towns. The most distressing outcome of the disease was that the doctors were as ignorant at the end of the epidemic as they had been at the beginning.

While the medical profession argued and attacked each other's ideas on the effectiveness of burning barrels of tar, washing houses with chlorine, and the wearing of thick flannel cholera belts, the disease claimed yet more victims. Scarcely two doctors agreed and in their ignorance many were driven into their laboratories to busy themselves over the microscope. In their desperation, strange connections were made between observations and the disease, and dangerous remedies were suggested. One doctor noted how a fly crawled out of a victim's eye, and a German doctor went to the length of suggesting the use of large quantities of arsenic as a cure.

Cholera continued its dark, steady advance through Britain. On 10 February, two days after a Fast Day had taken place to plead with God to help stop the disease, cholera appeared in London. Wherever the disease struck, it dragged into the daylight the poverty which existed everywhere. No place could escape.

By the end of 1832 the sufferings of most parts of the British Isles were slowly coming to an end. Out of a total population of 14 million some 21 882 people had died. As the first wave of the disease worked itself out, people could breathe again and feel safe – so safe that they felt there was no need to keep the Boards of Health. The Indian Cholera, however, was merely sleeping and the squalor on which it fed remained. The cholera giant was to reawaken in 1848.

THE NEED TO ACT

INVASION!
Three further Cholera epidemics followed the outbreak of 1831–2

1848

During the hot season the sleeping disease reawoke, this time in Afghanistan. It now burst out with new energy. Cholera followed the same sinister path across Europe and, sadly, nothing had changed.

On 22 September 1848 the first cholera victim was diagnosed in Britain. The disease had probably been carried by a sailor from Hamburg, Germany.

In December, *The Times* newspaper reported that when some people were still denying that cholera existed, 180 children out of 1 400 died in Tooting Poor House, where pauper children were dumped. The manager, who was put on trial for murder, was set free as the judge considered that the children would have died anyway.

Total deaths: 72 000

1853

Florence Nightingale, a young nurse of 33 working in the Middlesex Hospital, London, was put in charge of the cholera patients who were arriving every half hour. She described one case in particular:

The prostitutes came in perpetually, poor creatures staggering off their

beat: it took worse hold on them than on any. One poor girl, loathesomely filthy, came in and was dead in four hours. I held her in my arms and heard her saying something: 'Pray God that you may never be in the despair I am in at this time.'

Total deaths: 30 000

1866

On Wednesday 27 September a fatal case of Cholera was reported at Southampton. Little appeared to have changed. Gas workmen claimed that the gas protected them from the disease. Post Office sorters took a drink of orange peel and diluted sulphuric acid. Postmen who delivered letters to cholera districts were given 'cholera candy' – candy mixed with opium!

Total deaths: 18 000

Towards a Public Health Act

Cholera had invaded Britain four times by 1866. Its devastating effects were additional to other common killer diseases, such as tuberculosis, diphtheria, enteric fever and smallpox, which thrived in the towns. Gradually, concern grew and, although many people did not seem to learn any lessons from the cholera outbreaks, there were a few who did. The 'sanitary idea' of cleaning up the towns caught the imagination of these people. For example, in 1833, after the first cholera epidemic had died down, 44 doctors in Leeds called for a 'General Act of Parliament for sewering, draining, cleaning and paving' all large towns.

The crusader who was eventually to achieve this was Edwin Chadwick, a quarrelsome individual who made many enemies. Chadwick wanted to find ways of reducing the huge expense of keeping the poor in workhouses. He realised that poverty left people open to illness and death. Illness worsened poverty and the death of the family breadwinner could leave a mother and her children with no means of support. If living conditions could be improved, illness would lessen and less money would be needed to look after the poor.

After a very bad outbreak of typhus fever in 1838, Chadwick set up a three-man team to investigate how the poor of London lived. The members were Dr Neil Arnott, an expert on ventilation; Dr James Kay, a doctor who had worked in the poorest part of Manchester; and Dr Southwood Smith, a doctor at the London Fever Hospital.

Question
Why would the team of investigators need an expert on ventilation?

Edwin Chadwick

Like a team of detectives the doctors toured some of the worst parts of London and uncovered the terrible struggle for survival. In 1839 they published their report; they insisted that the problem was so huge that only the government could change things.

At first the government ignored their findings but then demanded a further report. This time it was to cover the whole country. Chadwick set about the job with great enthusiasm; he was determined that this time no one would be able to ignore the facts. He sent out questionnaires to many medical officers of health. Often he would carry out interviews himself, anxious to discover all the information necessary to prove the need for public health laws.

In his report Chadwick did not hold back, but hit out at the rich and powerful, whom he blamed for doing so little. His report, published at his own expense, was full of facts and vivid stories of the sufferings of the poor. No one who read it could avoid its terrible conclusions:

Doré's Bluegate Fields *shows poverty and despair in Victorian London*

That the various forms of epidemic disease ... amongst the labouring classes [are caused by] atmospheric impurities produced by decomposing animal and vegetable substances, by damp and filth, and close overcrowded buildings.

That the formation of all habits of cleanliness is obstructed by defective supplies of water....

That the annual loss of life from filth and bad ventilation are greater than the loss from death or wounds in any wars in which the country has been engaged in modern times.

less susceptible of moral influences: more likely to produce criminals

That the population so exposed [to bad living conditions] is less susceptible of moral influences....

be [a] gain: save money

That the expense of public drainage [and] supplies of water ... would be [a] gain by diminishing the existing charges [resulting from] sickness and mortality....

corporation: body of people responsible for running a town

We do not shrink from saying that the responsibility for this loss of life rests mainly upon those who have the greatest power to remove it – the corporation.... They can get powers which will enable them to prohibit back to back houses and cellar dwellings; to insist that all houses shall be connected with the new drainage. They could appoint a medical officer, whose business would be to ascertain ... the special causes of sickness....

The Report on the Sanitary Condition of the Labouring Population of Great Britain, 1842

Questions
1 Which group of people was most affected by disease?
2 According to Chadwick, how was disease spread?

3 What effect did Chadwick think the lack of sanitation had on the labouring population?
4 What was his main argument for recommending public health laws?
5 What powers did he think should be given to town corporations?
6 Who would provide the money for the corporation? Which group of people would be likely, therefore, to oppose Chadwick's ideas?
7 This report was an official document. Was it likely to be more reliable than a personal one such as a letter or diary?

So important was Chadwick's report that it became a best seller! Two more reports followed in 1844 and 1845, repeating the conclusions reached by Chadwick. A group of doctors and other eminent men formed the 'Health of Towns Association' to persuade the government to act.

In 1847 Lord Morpeth introduced a Public Health Bill into Parliament. However, its opponents argued against it so well that the bill was set aside. These opponents were nicknamed 'The Dirty Party'. Some of their arguments are listed below. Copy out the table and, bearing in mind the earlier chapters as well as Chadwick's report, write in the answers you would produce as a member of the 'Sanitary Party':

The Dirty Party	*The Sanitary Party*
1 Cleaning up the towns would cost too much!	
2 It is not the government's job to clean up the towns	
3 The poor should do something to help themselves	
4 The poor do not have a vote. Why should we do anything for them?	
5 Giving the government power to clean up the towns would make the State too powerful!	

Lord Morpeth tried again with a second bill in February 1848 and this time he was better prepared. The most powerful argument on his side, though, was the menace of cholera moving across Europe once again. On 31 August 1848 the government reached a milestone in the history of public health, when the Public Health Act was passed. Its main parts were:

1 A National Central Board of Health for England and Wales, except London, was set up, consisting of three members. The Board was to be in force for five years.
2 Towns with a death rate of 23 per 1 000 or above were forced to set up a Local Board of Health.
3 Other towns could set up a Board of Health if one tenth of the ratepayers demanded it and the Central Board of Health agreed.
4 The Local Board of Health had to appoint a surveyor and inspector of Nuisances; it had to lay down sewers, cleanse streets, remove rubbish and provide a water supply.
5 A Board of Health could appoint a Medical Officer of Health, pave the streets and even create parks.

Nuisances: public health hazards

There were three major weaknesses in the Act: the most obvious was that the Act was permissive. In other words, a town was not forced to set up a Board of Health unless its death rate was high.

Questions
1 What were the other two major weaknesses?
2 Look back to the arguments of 'The Dirty Party'. How do these arguments help to explain the weakness of the 1848 Act?

Increasing government involvement
Whether or not the 1848 Public Health Act would be successful remained to be seen. It had weaknesses, but the original Central Board of Health had a strong team: Lord Morpeth, Lord Ashley and Chadwick himself. Dr Southwood Smith, a fierce campaigner to improve public health, was its chief medical officer. The Act was opposed by several groups in Britain: water companies, town corporations, property owners and many ratepayers all felt that the government was meddling in matters which did not concern it. Look at this excerpt from a journal for engineers:

> ... *[Chadwick] was determined that the British world should be clean and live a century, but on one condition only – that they consented to purchase the real patent Chadwickian soap, the Chadwickian officially-gathered soft water and the true impermeable telescopic earthware pipes, and when they did die, were interred by his official undertakers in the Chadwickian necropolis.*
>
> *Engineers and Officials,* 1856

impermeable: watertight

necropolis: city of the dead

42

Question
Of what is Chadwick being accused in this extract?

It is with pride, therefore, I repeat, that whatever may be the case in the country (where I regret to see the hateful Public Health Act seems to be extending its ravages), in London we are enjoying the enormous privilege of self-government, and that if the epidemic Cholera should visit us again, we may confidently show him to his old haunts of 1832 and 1849, and so convince him that, in this free country, he, too, is at liberty 'TO DO WHAT HE LIKES WITH HIS OWN'.

Punch, 1852

Questions
1 Is this extract for or against Chadwick's public health efforts?
2 How does the article make its point to the reader? How would you describe its attitude?

Sir John Simon

Chadwick's drive and determination had placed the problem of public health on the conscience of the government. However, he was occasionally wrong in medical matters. In 1848, for example, he was responsible for getting sewers flushed into the Thames, which was the source of London's drinking water. He came under increasing attack from people and groups he had offended. In 1853 he was forced to resign and in 1858 the Central Board of Health was scrapped.

The Board's medical duties were taken over by the Privy Council (the sovereign's personal advisers), which appointed Sir John Simon as its Chief Medical Officer. Sir John had been responsible for considerable work in London, transforming the capital into a good example of local government by getting a private Act of Parliament passed, within the rules set out in the 1848 Act, and cleaning up many bad areas of the city. His activity prompted the government to extend local and central powers: in 1855 the Privy Council was empowered to take action when any 'formidable' epidemic arose in any part of the country; and in 1860 an Act empowered local boards to appoint experts who could check on articles of food being sold – fines and penalties could be imposed if food was found to contain inferior materials.

In 1868 local boards were empowered to regulate conditions in workmen's lodgings. Overall, however, there was still no central government control. In 1870 out of 59 towns investigated, only 18 had appointed permanent Medical Officers of Health, and their salaries varied from £1 000 p.a. to 50p per day for a three-month period. Not surprisingly, the death rate varied little:

Date	Deaths per 1 000 of population England and Wales	Scotland	Deaths of infants under one year per 1 000 (live births) England and Wales	Scotland
1858	23.1	23.1	151	121
1859	22.4	20.3	153	108
1860	21.2	22.3	148	127
1861	21.6	20.3	153	111
1862	21.4	21.7	142	117
1863	23.0	22.9	149	120
1864	23.7	23.6	153	126
1865	23.2	22.3	160	125
1866	23.4	22.7	160	122
1867	21.7	21.3	153	119
1868	21.8	21.2	155	118
1869	22.3	23.0	156	129
1870	22.9	22.2	160	123
1871	22.6	22.2	158	130

Question

Apart from the ineffectiveness of the 1848 Act, what other factors would continue to cause high death rates in towns?

Using the evidence: further reasons for government action

After the 1848 Public Health Act had been passed, other factors began to work towards convincing the government that local authorities needed to be compelled to clean up their towns:

A   In 1867 working men in the towns were given the vote.

cajoled: persuaded

> *. . . the working men of England, finding themselves in a full majority . . . will awake to a full sense of their power. They will say, 'we can do better for ourselves. Don't let us be any longer cajoled at elections. Let us shop for ourselves . . . we have our trade unions: we have our leaders all ready. . . .'*
> The Reform Bill of 1866: Robert Lowe's speech, 13 March

1   What does Lowe suggest that working men would be able to do once they had the vote?
2   Why would the government be keen to pass laws which were of benefit to the working men?

B   From 1836 onwards all births and deaths had to be officially registered. William Farr was in charge of the Register from 1839. In 1840 he described the importance of the collection of facts and figures about births and deaths in a letter to a friend:

The simple process of comparing the deaths in a given time out of a given number living is a modern discovery. It was probably not generally known ... that the main duration of life was from 25 to 30 years in the east districts, and from 40 to 50 years in the north and west districts of the metropolis.

1 What did the registration of births and deaths provide the government with for the first time?
2 What would the government be able to assess very accurately?
3 What would the government be unable to ignore?

C By the 1860s Britain was no longer the only country experiencing an Industrial Revolution. Products from other countries such as Prussia (later known as Germany) were beginning to compete with those made in Britain. A healthy work-force became a necessity:

The wealth of the country lies not only in its material resources but in the strong limbs of its people. All these are dependent on health, without which this country would be hard pressed by other and perhaps healthier countries.

The Times, 18 July 1881

1 In the nineteenth century it was generally acknowledged that the government's job was to guard the interests of the nation against other countries. How could you argue from the above extract that by extending its authority into public health, the government was acting wisely and properly?

D By 1870 the medical profession was beginning to pay attention to the discoveries of Louis Pasteur, the French chemist. In public experiments he had demonstrated clearly that:

(i)   The air contains living microbes or germs.
(ii) The microbes are distributed at random in the air.
(iii) Many microbes cause decay and spread disease.
(iv) Microbes could be killed by boiling the liquid in which they settled and thrived.

A cartoon from Punch, *showing 'microbes' in a drop of London water*

1 Nineteenth century doctors took for granted the theory of 'spontaneous generation', which was that germs were the result of disease and that they simply grew out of rotting or diseased flesh. How had Pasteur shown this theory to be wrong?
2 What conclusion about the need for clean surroundings might a Board of Health draw from Pasteur's discovery?

Together these factors built up an awareness in the government that public health was a matter which could no longer be ignored. Many of the beneficial measures taken by the government since 1848 had caused much confusion. In 1869 the government appointed the Royal Sanitary Commission to sort out the various Acts of Parliament and matters of importance in public health. In 1875 *The Times* newspaper summarised what the Commission found:

> *No less than 29 sanitary measures have been enacted since the Health of towns Commission of 1846. . . . These Acts displayed much redundancy and . . . confusion. They had been made at different times, by various hands. . . . Some were permissive, some compulsory. . . .*

The result of the Royal Commission was that the Government acted upon its recommendations and passed the Public Health Act of 1875, which made it compulsory for local authorities to ensure that proper standards of public health were maintained by officially appointed and paid officers. This Act is still the basis of health regulations today. In addition, the government passed the Artisans' Dwellings Act in 1875, recognising the importance it needed to attach to making sure that people were adequately housed. The following extracts are from the introduction to the Act:

> *. . . we have endeavoured to pass laws to prevent overcrowding in dwelling houses. . . . We have also passed Acts enabling Corporations to give up their land and borrow money in order to erect dwelling houses for the working classes. We have also passed an Act . . . enabling local authorities to pull down such houses as are absolutely unfit for human habitation. . . . When we remember that the growth of London has advanced during the last twenty years at the rate of 40 000 each year, it is clear that much more must be done if we wish to reach the rest of the evil. . . .*

> *I would ask [people to remember] that health is actual wealth.*

> *We have . . . to ask ourselves whether we can give the children of the working classes an equal chance of growing up to healthy manhood and womanhood. The causes of the present loss of life are not far to seek . . . it is not simply that houses are overcrowded . . . but districts are overcrowded. . . .*

Questions
1 In spite of the number of Acts of Parliament, why were housing conditions still so terrible?
2 How does the writer guarantee to the working classes that they shall have a healthy environment?

The Artisans' Dwellings Act gave local authorities the power to make compulsory purchases of slum properties. Owners of such properties, who were forced to sell to the authorities, received compensation.

The State had finally accepted responsibility for providing everyone with healthy surroundings. But that was not the end of the story – it was not until the twentieth century that the clearance of slums was actually achieved on a massive scale. 1875 was a beginning: the State had seen the connection between environment and disease and had accepted responsibility for public health.

EPILOGUE

Cholera was mainly responsible for raising the whole issue of public health. What became of the disease itself?

It was not until 1883 that the actual microbe was identified by a German doctor, Robert Koch. But the manner in which the germ spread had been discovered long before by a doctor in England.

Dr John Snow was born in York, in 1813. The son of a farmer, he was apprenticed to a surgeon in Newcastle upon Tyne at the age of 14. His first-hand experience of cholera was gained at Killingworth Colliery in 1831, where he fought the disease single-handed. Five years later he set out on foot for London. After qualifying as a member of the Royal College of Surgeons, he set up a practice in Soho.

Snow was a serious-minded young man. His Soho practice did not do well, mainly because, as a friend wrote, 'he had no personal introduction to the bedsides of dowagers and there was not the least element of quackery in his treatment'. But he did make a name for himself after the introduction of anaesthetics, when he administered chloroform to Queen Victoria to ease the pain of childbirth.

In the 1848 cholera outbreak Snow turned his attention to the problem of the disease once more. He doubted the miasmists' theory that the disease was spread through the air, suspecting instead that it was transmitted through the water supply. Snow published his ideas in 1849. His theory was not widely accepted. The miasmists were all-powerful at this time and Snow was shy and unambitious.

The 1855 edition of Snow's book was much more detailed. He described how cholera spread fastest among the poor, because the areas of the houses where food was prepared and eaten were cramped. He also described how cholera was spread through water that was drawn from polluted rivers and then used for drinking and cooking.

Snow died in 1858. For his work on cholera he received neither fame nor reward. Instead he lost £200 by having his book published at his own expense.

Dr John Snow

47

INDEX